Andrew Carnegie

Andrew Carnegie

Builder of Libraries

by Charnan Simon

Children's Press®
A Division of Grolier Publishing
New York London Hong Kong Sydney
Danbury, Connecticut

Photo Credits

Photographs ©: Archive Photos: cover, 16, 19; Boston Public Library: 2; Brown Brothers: 8, 17, 25, 32, 33, 39, 40, 44; Carnegie Library of Pittsburgh: 23, 34, 37, 43 top, 43 bottom; Corbis-Bettmann: 3, 11, 13, 26; Culver Pictures: 45; Library of Congress: 27; Metro Government of Nashville,: 43 center (Gary Layda); Monkmeyer Press: 9 (Merrim); Museum of the City of New York/Archive Photos: 7; North Wind Picture Archives: 14, 35; Photo Researchers: 42 (Bachmann); Superstock, Inc.: back cover, 20.

Author photo ©: Tom Kazunas.

Library of Congress Cataloging-in-Publication Data

Simon, Charnan.
    Andrew Carnegie : builder of libraries / by Charnan Simon.
       p. cm. — (Community builders)
    Includes bibliographical references and index.
    Summary: Describes the efforts of Andrew Carnegie to build public libraries as a way of improving community life in Pittsburgh and other places.
    ISBN: 0-516-20289-8 (lib. bdg.)   0-516-26131-2 (pbk.)
    1. Carnegie libraries—United States—History—19th century—Juvenile literature.   2. Carnegie libraries—United States—History—20th century—Juvenile literature.   3. Carnegie, Andrew, 1835-1919—Juvenile literature. [1. Public libraries—History. 2. Carnegie, Andrew, 1835-1919.] I. Title. II. Series: Simon, Charnan. Community builders.
Z731.S56 1997
027.473—DC20   96-31027
                                                    CIP
                                                     AC

Contents

Chapter ONE

Library Day

Does your community have a library? Can you imagine what your community would be like without one? A little more than a hundred years ago, most towns didn't have free public libraries. There was no such thing as "borrowing" books. Usually, only rich people read books because they were the only people who could afford to buy them.

A man named Andrew Carnegie believed that people should be able to get books anytime they wanted. When Andrew was a poor boy growing up in Pittsburgh, Pennsylvania, in the 1850s, there were no public libraries. But there was a man in Pittsburgh who allowed young working boys to read the books in his own private library. Throughout his

6

Andrew Carnegie

life, Andrew Carnegie remembered the wonderful feeling he had when he walked into that library to pick out a book. It was a feeling he wanted other young people to experience.

From a young age, Andrew Carnegie knew that reading was an important part of a person's education.

Andrew Carnegie grew up to be one of the richest men in the United States. But he never forgot what it was like to be poor and to be hungry for books. In his later years, Andrew gave away almost as much money as he had earned during his lifetime. Much of his money went to start public libraries in towns all over the world. Perhaps you borrowed this very book from an Andrew Carnegie library.

If you borrowed this book from a public library, you didn't have to pay any money for it. Adults pay for libraries the same way they pay for schools and highways, by paying taxes. But when you step up to the checkout counter of your neighborhood library, you don't have to pay a penny (unless you have some fines for overdue books). One of the greatest parts of the American library system is that anyone can visit the library.

8

How to Borrow a Book

Libraries are a great source for informative and entertaining books.

Did you check out this book from your public library? If so, you joined the millions of Americans who use libraries every year. Anyone (students, parents, teachers, toddlers) can borrow a book from the library. It's easy! As soon as you can write your name, you can get your own library card. With it, you can borrow library books as often as you like. You just pick out your favorite titles, show the librarian your card, and head home for some great reading.

A Boy from Dunfermline

Andrew Carnegie was born in the snug little town of Dunfermline, Scotland, on November 25, 1835. Andrew's father, William, was a linen weaver. Like many of the men in Dunfermline, he worked at a hand-powered loom in his home. The weavers of Dunfermline produced beautiful linen tablecloths. These tablecloths were famous throughout the world.

It wasn't easy to earn a living in Scotland in 1835. The Industrial Revolution was in full swing. Machines in factories could make cloth faster and

Andrew Carnegie's birthplace in Dunfermline,
Scotland, has been preserved as a museum.

The Industrial Revolution

The Industrial Revolution began in England during the 1700s. Before the Industrial Revolution, most people lived on farms and in small towns. Skilled craftspeople such as William Carnegie worked out of their homes on hand-powered machines. But during the Industrial Revolution, machines powered by steam and other energy sources came into use. People moved to the cities to work in factories filled with these new machines. Hand weavers and other skilled workers often went out of business because their goods were more expensive than factory-made goods.

During the Industrial Revolution, factories manufactured goods faster and cheaper than skilled workers could.

cheaper than hand weavers could. All over Scotland weavers feared that they would lose their jobs.

By 1848, Andrew Carnegie's father knew that he could no longer support his family in Dunfermline. The new cotton factory at the edge of town produced cloth much faster than he could on his handloom. With deep sadness, the Carnegie family decided to leave Scotland. They hoped that life would be better for them in the "land of opportunity" across the Atlantic Ocean—the United States of America.

Adventures in a New Land

Pittsburgh, Pennsylvania, about 1850

Andrew Carnegie and his family arrived in the United States and settled in the city of Pittsburgh, Pennsylvania. Two of Andrew's aunts were already living in Pittsburgh. There was also a large Scottish community that had been established. This helped the Carnegies to feel at home.

14

Pittsburgh, Pennsylvania

Pittsburgh is located in the southwestern part of Pennsylvania. There, the Allegheny and Monongahela Rivers join to form the Ohio River. Today, Pittsburgh is one of the greatest steelmaking centers in the world, and the area is home to more than two million people.

Pittsburgh

William Carnegie didn't waste any time setting up his loom in Pittsburgh. But he soon found that here, too, factory-made goods were much less expensive than handmade items. Working in the United States was as difficult as working in Scotland. William grew discouraged as he sold fewer and fewer tablecloths.

Soon after settling in Pennsylvania, William Carnegie realized that the goods being made in nearby factories were more popular than his handmade products.

Andrew Carnegie was twelve years old when his family settled in Pittsburgh. In those days, twelve-year-old boys and girls were considered old enough to help support their families. Andrew quickly found a job in a cotton factory in Pittsburgh. The work was difficult and the hours were long. Andrew didn't get paid much money, either. He earned only $1.20 a week. Still, Andrew was earning money for the first time in his life. It was a feeling he liked very much.

16

The Industrial Revolution made life difficult for William Carnegie. But it also made life exciting for young Andrew. The United States was growing fast in the middle of the 1800s. New inventions such as the telegraph and the railroads offered many opportunities for energetic, intelligent boys like Andrew Carnegie.

Andrew's first big opportunity came when he was offered a job as a messenger in a telegraph office. Andrew didn't hesitate to accept the job. He thought that delivering messages to Pittsburgh's most important citizens would be much better than working hard all day in a dark factory.

In the 1850s, children as young as twelve worked to support their families. Like Andrew Carnegie, this boy delivered messages for a telegraph company.

What Is a Telegraph?

The telegraph was invented by Samuel Morse in 1837. It is a machine used to send messages over long distances. A code, called Morse Code, is made up of signals that are sent over wires or radio.

"Young Andy," as he came to be known around Pittsburgh, was hardworking and smart. He quickly memorized all the streets in Pittsburgh. He also found the fastest routes for delivering his messages. Andy taught himself how to send and receive messages over the telegraph wires. Before long, he was promoted to telegraph operator. Andy was earning twenty-five dollars a month.

Working in the telegraph office gave Andy a chance to meet Pittsburgh's best-known business-people. One of them, Thomas Scott, was superinten-

Morse Code was transported by telegraph and translated into words by workers who listened to the signals.

dent of the Western Division of the Pennsylvania Railroad. Mr. Scott liked Andy's energy, spirit, and ambition. He liked it so much that he offered Andy a job as his personal assistant.

**Rapidly expanding railroads made
travel, transportation, and settlement
of the West possible.**

It was another wonderful opportunity for Andrew Carnegie. He learned that railroads were important to the growth of the United States. More people were moving to the United States from Europe. Some of these people settled in the East to work in factories. Some of them traveled in covered wagons to settle in the West. Soon those westward pioneers would need supplies made by factories in the East. Then the factories would need raw materials from the West. Raw materials are substances such as wood, oil, and stone that are turned into useful products. How would these supplies and raw materials go back and forth, from East to West? Andrew was sure that railroads were the answer.

Andrew Carnegie began working for Thomas Scott in 1853. He was seventeen years old. He had been in the United States for a little more than four years, and he was now earning thirty-five dollars a month. In 1859, Thomas Scott became vice president of the Pennsylvania Railroad. Andrew Carnegie took his place as superintendent of the Western Division of the railroad. He was twenty-four years old.

The War Between the States

The Civil War lasted from 1861 to 1865. The Southern (Confederate) states fought to save their right to own slaves. They were also fighting to save their agricultural (farming) way of life. The Northern (Union) states wanted to end slavery.

Andrew Carnegie didn't fight in the Civil War. But his work on the telegraph systems and the railroads made important contributions to the Northern states' victory. The telegraph helped President Abraham Lincoln communicate with army officers who were hundreds of miles apart. The railroads carried soldiers and supplies much more quickly than horses and wagons could have.

It was a big promotion for Andrew. He bought a comfortable house in Pittsburgh, where he lived with his mother and his sixteen-year-old brother, Tom. Andrew's only regret was that his father had already died, and he couldn't share in Andrew's success.

When the Civil War began in 1861, Thomas Scott and Andrew Carnegie went to Washington, D.C., to help the Union army by restoring all the railroads and telegraph systems. It was quite a challenge for Andrew, but he liked challenges!

By the time Andrew was twenty-four years old, he was the superintendent of the Western Division of the Pennsylvania Railroad.

Andrew Carnegie worked for the Pennsylvania Railroad until just before the Civil War ended in 1865. Then, in a move that surprised everyone, he quit his job at the railroad. It was time for new adventures.

Chapter FOUR

"Determined to Make a Fortune"

While Andrew Carnegie was working for the Pennsylvania Railroad, he also earned money in other ways. For example, Andrew saw how quickly railroad tracks were being built across the United States. Soon it would be possible for people to ride trains from one end of the country to the other. Andrew didn't think that people would want to sit up in their seats for an entire trip because some trips could take many days. So Andrew became

24

Long train trips became so popular that Andrew invested
in a company that made railroad cars for travelers to sleep in.

The Union Pacific and Central Pacific Railroads
celebrate their meeting at Promontory Summit, Utah.

The Transcontinental Railroad

During the 1860s, the United States was expanding quickly. Railroads became a popular way to travel. President Abraham Lincoln thought that an east-west railroad route stretching across the country was a good idea. In 1862, Lincoln signed the Railroad Act, which allowed for two companies to begin building the first transcontinental railroad. In 1863, the Union Pacific Railroad started building west from Omaha, Nebraska. The Central Pacific Railroad started building east from Sacramento, California. The two tracks were joined together on May 10, 1869, at Promontory Summit, Utah.

Although the Civil War demanded much of Lincoln's attention, he also was concerned with the growth of the United States.

excited when he heard about a company that was building railroad cars for passengers to sleep in.

Andrew decided he would invest money in the company that made these sleeping cars. In return, every time one of the cars was sold, Andrew would earn some money back. Andrew thought that a lot of sleeping cars would be sold. He also thought that he would make a lot of money. He was right.

Andrew used the money he earned from sleeping cars to invest in other projects. As a railroad man, he knew that wooden railway bridges were often destroyed by fires or washed away by floods. Andrew thought that iron bridges would be safer, so he started the Keystone Bridge Company. This company built iron bridges all across the United States. And Andrew made money on every one.

Andrew Carnegie also invested in oil wells. Before the Industrial Revolution, no one had much use for oil. But Andrew could see that the new factories would need oil to fuel their machines. He began to buy oil wells in Pennsylvania and Ohio. Before long, Andrew was very rich.

Oil

The oil industry began in the United States in 1859, when Edwin L. Drake drilled an oil well in Titusville, Pennsylvania. Today, most of the oil in the United States is found in Texas, Alaska, and California. Oil is one of the most important natural resources in the world. It is found in rocks that are deep below the earth's surface. Oil is used to power machines such as cars, trucks, trains, tractors, and lawn mowers. Many homes, businesses, and factories use oil for heat and electricity.

One reason that Andrew Carnegie was so successful was that he wasn't afraid to take risks. He was willing to invest his money on products and inventions that he thought would become popular.

Andrew Carnegie was also successful because he insisted that things be done correctly—at every stage of every project. Quality mattered to Andrew. He gave all of his projects his personal attention. He expected the people who worked with him to do the same. For example, when Andrew started building iron bridges, he realized that the only way to make sure he was getting the best quality iron was to manufacture it himself. So Andrew began buying and building iron mills. Now he could always have just the kind of high-quality iron he wanted.

Andrew also paid strict attention to how much money it cost to manufacture iron. Some mill owners didn't know whether they were making money or losing money until they added up all their bills at the end of the year. This would never do for Andrew Carnegie! He introduced a system that made sure that no money or materials were wasted in his mills.

By 1865, Andrew was earning so much that he quit the railroad. He didn't want to work for other people anymore. He wanted to be his own boss. In his auto-biography, he wrote, "I was determined to make a fortune and I saw no means of doing this honestly at any salary the railroad company could afford to give. [From then on] I never worked for a salary."

After Andrew left the Pennsylvania Railroad, he decided to move from Pittsburgh to New York City. New York City was the financial center of the country. Many of the country's biggest banks were located there. Since Andrew was now involved in projects that involved huge sums of money, he felt that it was important to be near those large banks. He decided that his brother, Tom, could manage the mills in Pittsburgh.

Even though Andrew no longer lived in Pittsburgh, his first interests were always his hometown iron mills. Andrew stayed involved by hiring the best workers and making the best deals. He always kept his eyes and ears open for new ways to make the best iron.

Soon even the best iron wasn't good enough for the country's building needs. Steel was much stronger and easier to work with than iron. So

Andrew Carnegie decided to build the largest and most modern steel mill in the United States. It was called the Edgar Thomson Steel Works. It was located just outside of Pittsburgh.

Other steel mills followed. Each one made more money than the last. By 1890, Andrew Carnegie had made Pittsburgh the leading steel and iron manufacturing city in the country. Eventually, more than fifteen thousand people would work for the Carnegie Steel Company.

Andrew Carnegie had a good reputation as a fair man to work for. He liked and respected his workers. He paid them as much as other factory owners

**The Edgar Thomson Steel Works,
near Pittsburgh, Pennsylvania**

Andrew moved from Pittsburgh to New York City to be closer to the large banks that he did business with.

paid their employees. But in 1892, the workers at Carnegie's Homestead Steel Works went on strike. They refused to work until they were paid more money. As a result of the Homestead Steelworkers' Strike, Carnegie's reputation as a fair boss suffered.

The Carnegie Steel Company

The Homestead Steelworkers' Strike

Andrew Carnegie was traveling in Scotland when the workers in his company went on strike. The manager in charge of the Homestead Steel Works called in detectives with guns to help handle the strike. A fight broke out. Eighteen people were killed and many more were injured. It was the worst fight between workers and their bosses in United States history.

Giving Away a Fortune

By 1900, the Carnegie Steel Company was making more than $40 million every year. Andrew Carnegie enjoyed being a manufacturer and businessman, but he decided that it was time for another change. In January 1900, Andrew sold his entire iron and steel empire for $250 million. He was sixty-five years old at the time and had a fortune that came to $300 million. He spent the rest of his life giving his fortune away.

Andrew Carnegie believed that rich people shouldn't spend all their money on themselves. He

Andrew's charitable contributions included founding the Carnegie Technical Schools, where students could learn science, engineering, and industrial arts.

thought that they should help their communities by giving their money to good causes. Andrew disapproved of rich people who died without giving away any of their money.

Andrew believed that many of the world's problems came about because people didn't have enough education. All of his life, he had tried to educate himself by reading books and by talking to educated people. He was sorry that he had never been able to go to college. So one of the first things he did was give large sums of money to schools and colleges around the country.

Andrew Carnegie also gave money to help retired workers who couldn't afford to buy much. He supported peace organizations around the world. He established a Hero Fund to reward ordinary people who act like heroes in their everyday lives. He paid doctors and scientists to look for cures for terrible diseases. As a boy in Scotland, Andrew had loved organ music. He paid for more than eight thousand church organs in the United States, Canada, and Great Britain. And Andrew Carnegie didn't forget Pittsburgh. In his adopted hometown, he donated the money that was needed to build two colleges, an art gallery, a museum, a concert hall, and a symphony orchestra!

The back of
the Hero Fund
medal reads,
"Greater love
hath no man than
this, that a man
lay down his life
for his friends."

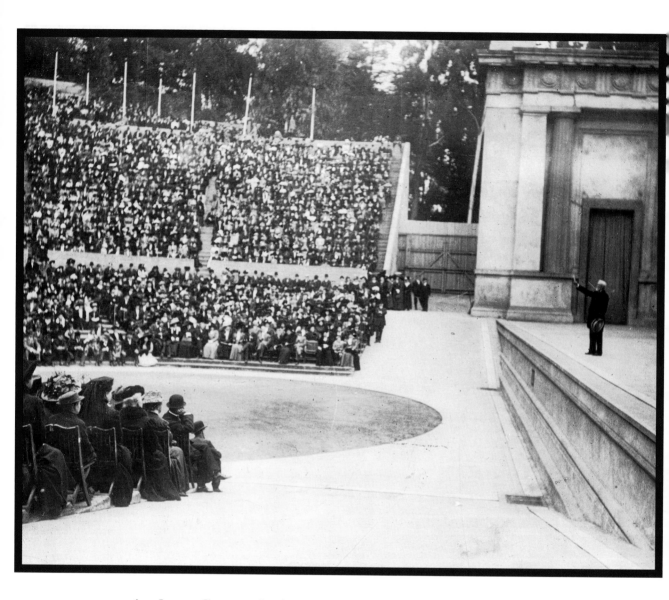

Andrew Carnegie (onstage) addresses an audience
at the University of California following the dedication
of another Carnegie-funded library.

Despite Andrew's efforts to give away all of his money, he still had a lot left. So he set up the Carnegie Corporation. This corporation would keep giving away Andrew's money even after he died. It would support schools, libraries, and scientific research. Today, the Carnegie Corporation is still giving money to worthy causes.

Andrew Carnegie gave away hundreds of millions of dollars. He supported many great causes. But he may be best remembered for the Andrew Carnegie libraries he started around the world.

Andrew Carnegie got the idea for starting libraries when he was a poor telegraph messenger boy in Pittsburgh. A man there named Colonel James Anderson allowed working boys to borrow books from his personal library. Every Saturday, boys such as Andrew Carnegie would go to Colonel Anderson's home and choose a book to read. Andrew never forgot the generous man who helped him to become better educated.

So later in life, Andrew paid for libraries to be built. Any town that asked for one could have an

Andrew Carnegie library built for free. All Andrew asked for in return was that the community keep the library filled with books for people to borrow.

As word spread, communities around the United States—and then around the world—began asking for Andrew Carnegie libraries. From California to Canada, from Australia to Alabama, towns and cities everywhere began building libraries for all kinds of people to enjoy. In all, Andrew Carnegie paid for 2,811 libraries.

Andrew died peacefully in his sleep on August 11, 1919. But his generosity and dedication to educating others lives on.

Andrew Carnegie believed that all children should have the same access to books that he had.

Carnegie libraries were built
all over the world. Although some
are no longer in use as libraries,
many of them still exist.

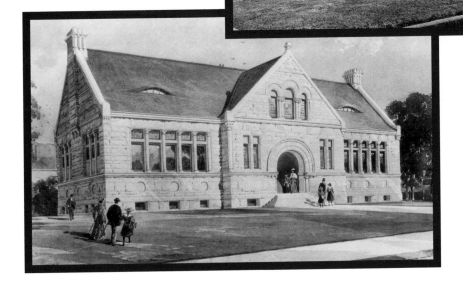

In Your Community

Today, some Andrew Carnegie libraries have been torn down to make room for new buildings. Others are still standing, but they are no longer being used as libraries. Throughout the world, though, many Andrew Carnegie libraries still exist.

Is there an Andrew Carnegie

Timeline

1835 — Andrew Carnegie is born on November 25 in Dunfermline, Scotland.

1848 — The Carnegie family settles in Pittsburgh, Pennsylvania.

1850 — Andrew begins work as a telegraph messenger boy.

1853 — Andrew becomes Thomas Scott's personal assistant on the Pennsylvania Railroad Company.

1859 — Andrew is named superintendent of the Western Division of the Pennsylvania Railroad.

1861 — The Civil War begins on April 12, and Andrew goes to Washington, D.C., to restore railways and telegraph lines for the Union army.

1865 — The Civil War ends on April 9.

1865 — Keystone Bridge Company is founded by Andrew Carnegie.

1865 — Andrew leaves the Pennsylvania Railroad Company to devote his time to his own businesses.

library in your community? What is it being used for? Find out the answers to these questions by visiting your library. The librarian can tell you if your library is a Carnegie library. The librarian can also tell you if there are any Carnegie libraries nearby. And while you're in the library—borrow a book or two!

Andrew forms a huge corporation called Carnegie Brothers & Company, Ltd. (later renamed Carnegie Steel Company).

The Homestead Steelworkers' Strike occurs, and Andrew's reputation as a fair man is damaged.

Andrew sells Carnegie Steel Company. He spends the rest of his life finding worthwhile ways to give away his huge personal fortune.

Andrew moves from Pittsburgh to New York City.

1867 — **1873** — **1881** — **1887** — **1892** — **1897** — **1900** — **1919**

Andrew begins building the Edgar Thomson Steel Works.

Andrew marries Louise Whitfield on April 22.

Andrew's only child, Margaret, is born in March.

Andrew Carnegie dies on August 11.

To Find Out More

Here are some additional resources to help you learn more about Andrew Carnegie's life, his work, and other topics mentioned in this book:

Books

Anderson, Peter. *The Transcontinental Railroad.* Children's Press, 1996.

Fradin, Dennis Brindell. *Pennsylvania.* Children's Press, 1994.

Rickard, Graham. *Oil.* Thomson Learning, 1993.

Organizations and Online Sites

Carnegie Corporation of New York
437 Madison Avenue
New York, NY 10022
http://www.carnegie.org/welcome.html

Carnegie Endowment for International Peace
2400 N Street, NW
Washington, DC 20037

Carnegie Hall
Take a virtual tour and learn the history of the most famous music hall in the world.
http://www.carnegiehall.org/

Carnegie Institution of Washington
1530 P Street, NW
Washington, DC 20005

The Carnegie (formerly Carnegie Institute)
4400 Forbes Avenue
Pittsburgh, PA 15213

The Carnegie Museum of Art
Information about the Carnegie Museum of Art, including links to the Carnegie Museum of Natural History.
http://www.clpgh.org/exhibit/neighborhoods/oakland/oak_centf.html

The Carnegie Science Center
One Allegheny Avenue
Pittsburgh, PA 15212
http://www.csc.clpgh.org

Index

About
the Author

Charnan Simon lives in Madison, Wisconsin, with her husband and her two daughters. She is a former editor at *Cricket* magazine, and sometimes works at a children's bookstore called Pooh Corner. But mainly she likes reading and writing books and spending time with her family.

When Ms. Simon was growing up in Walla Walla, Washington, she visited the Andrew Carnegie library at least once a week. The children's books were kept on the lower level, and the adult books were kept on the upper level. Ms. Simon couldn't wait until she was thirteen—old enough to borrow books from the upper level. Today, Walla Walla has a new library. The old Carnegie library has been made into the Carnegie Art Center.